50 FINDS FROM LINCOLNSHIRE

Objects from the Portable Antiquities Scheme

Adam Daubney

AMBERLEY

First published 2016

Amberley Publishing
The Hill, Stroud
Gloucestershire, GL5 4EP

www.amberley-books.com

Copyright © Adam Daubney, 2016

The right of Adam Daubney to be identified as the
Author of this work has been asserted in accordance
with the Copyrights, Designs and Patents Act 1988.

ISBN 978 1 4456 5811 7 (print)
ISBN 978 1 4456 5812 4 (ebook)

British Library Cataloguing in Publication Data.
A catalogue record for this book is available from
the British Library.

Typeset in 10pt on 13pt Celeste.
Typesetting by Amberley Publishing.
Printed in the UK.

Contents

Acknowledgements

This book is the result of over thirteen years of working for the Portable Antiquities Scheme. Over that time, an impressive number and variety of antiquities have crossed my desk and I have been fortunate to have a job that takes me deep into the Lincolnshire countryside. A great many conversations have occurred with finders, museum curators, local archaeologists, academics and family regarding finds, sites and the latest 'treasures' to have been found in the county. This book is a tribute to them, and I hope that in turn it will inspire a deeper sense of intrigue into our county's rich archaeological landscape. I wish to thank staff at Lincolnshire County Council for their support of the PAS, in particular Antony Lee, archaeology curator at the Collection, Alastair MacIntosh, Lincoln City Archaeologist, and staff in the Historic Environment Team, including Beryl Lott, Mark Bennet, Richard Watts, Louise Jennings, Jan Allen, Karen Waite, and Sarah Grundy. I also wish to thank colleagues at the British Museum and staff at the Portable Antiquities Scheme, past and present. Special thanks are due to Roger Bland, Michael Lewis, Sally Worrell, Helen Geake, John Naylor, Kevin Leahy, Geoff Egan†, Sam Moorhead, Vincent Drost and Denise Wilding. I am grateful to Michael and Diana Honeybone for their insights into Maurice Johnson and the Spalding Gentlemen's Society. Finally, thanks are offered to the finders of the fifty objects that make up this book; indeed, these thanks extend to all those who have made their finds available for recording.

The author and publisher would like to thank the following people/organisations for permission to use copyright material in this book: the majority of finds images are made available by the Portable Antiquities Scheme/Lincolnshire County Council. Images 7–9 are reproduced with the permission of the Spalding Gentlemen's Society. Images 59 and 60 are courtesy of the Trustees of the British Museum/Portable Antiquities Scheme. Special thanks are due to Dr John Esser for kind permission to reproduce images 17, 68, 69, 82, 83, 110, 111, 118 and 142. John's pictures capture the essence of the historic landscapes in which these fifty objects have been found.

Every attempt has been made to seek permission for copyright material used in this book. However, if we have inadvertently used copyright material without permission/ acknowledgement we apologise and will make the necessary correction at the first opportunity.

Foreword

The places in which we live and work have a long past, but one that is not always obvious in the landscape around us. This is a forgotten past. Most of us know little about the people who once lived in our communities fifty years ago, let alone 500, or even 5000 years past. Like us, they lived, played and worked here, in this place, but we know almost nothing of them ...

History books tell us about royalty, great lords and important churchmen, but most others are forgotten by time. The only evidence for many of these people is the objects that they left behind; sometimes buried on purpose, but more often lost by chance. Sometimes, through archaeological fieldwork, we can place these objects in a context that allows us to understand the past better, but nowadays excavation is mostly development-led, so only takes place when a new building, road or service pipe, is being constructed.

A unique way of understanding the past is through the finds recorded through the Portable Antiquities Scheme, of which those chosen here by Adam Daubney (Finds Liaison Officer for Lincolnshire) are just fifty of over 75,000 recorded on its database (www.finds.org.uk). In fact Adam is unique, not only recording a vast quantity of these finds himself, but also as he used this data as the basis of his PhD to understand the historic landscape of Lincolnshire better.

These finds are all discovered by the public, most by metal-detector users, searching in places archaeologists are unlikely to go or otherwise excavate. As such they provide important clues of underlying archaeology that (once recorded) help archaeologists understand our past – a past of the people, found by the people.

Some of these finds are truly magnificent, others less imposing. Yet, like pieces in a jigsaw puzzle they are often meaningless alone, but once placed together they paint a picture. These finds therefore allow us to understand the story of people who once lived here, in Lincolnshire.

Dr Michael Lewis
Head of Portable Antiquities & Treasure
British Museum

Preface

Britain, like most European countries, has seen an unprecedented amount of land given over to arable cultivation since the Second World War. This is especially the case in the East Midlands – and Lincolnshire in particular – which contain vast areas of premium-grade agricultural land. Arable practices such as deep ploughing, harrowing and pan-busting have caused the destruction of many archaeological sites, and this continues today at unprecedented levels: sites are becoming scatters, and scatters are being increasingly dispersed through processes such as ploughing. This is, of course, a tension experienced across the globe wherever archaeology and the plough collide.

Although archaeological sites are regularly ploughed across Europe, England and Wales stand out from most of other countries in one key regard: the use of metal detectors is legal, providing the landowner's permission has been granted and that the land is not protected, such as being classed as a Scheduled Ancient Monument. Other than finds that qualify under the Treasure Act (1996), the reporting of finds is entirely voluntary – a situation that would have resulted in a substantial loss of archaeological knowledge was it not for the Portable Antiquities Scheme (PAS). The PAS was established in 1997 as a way of mitigating this loss of knowledge by encouraging the reporting of finds. This work is carried out by a network of Finds Liaison Officers, funded mostly through the British Museum and various local partners. In Lincolnshire the Finds Liaison Officer (FLO) is hosted by Lincolnshire County Council, while the North Lincolnshire FLO is hosted by North Lincolnshire Council.

In 2014 the PAS recorded its millionth object – a late Roman *nummus*, which was one of a hoard of 22,000 Roman coins discovered at Seaton, Devon. Of the million or so finds recorded by the PAS, around 75,000 have been found in Lincolnshire, reported by over 2,200 individuals. These finds have been reported from all areas of the county, from the Isle of Axholme in the north-west, to the Wash in the south-east. These finds range from Lower Palaeolithic hand axes – evidence of the first humans in the region – through to post-medieval trade tokens. Crucially, 96 per cent of these finds have been recovered from the plough zone (the volume of soil under cultivation), where modern farming techniques and exposure to the elements puts them increasingly at risk of deterioration. The majority of finds have been reported by metal detectorists, but not all. Amazing discoveries have been reported by gardeners, dog walkers, builders and people just out enjoying the countryside.

Above: Deep scars caused by ploughing are visible across the floor of this Roman villa in Sudbrooke, near Lincoln.

New finds continue to be reported every day, though sadly many still go unreported. Those finders who have made their discoveries available for recording have helped to transform our understanding of the rural landscape. This book charts some of the best discoveries since 2003. It celebrates the diligence of those who have reported them, and highlights fifty instances where 'recording' has avoided the sort of erosion of knowledge described by Oliver in 1846:

> The city [Lincoln] is surrounded by vestiges of the highest antiquity, in the form of stone idols and tumuli, which are daily disappearing before the progress of agricultural improvements and every memorial of our remote ancestors ... will soon have entirely passed away.
>
> (Oliver 1846: vi)

Further information on each find in this book can be found on the PAS database www.finds.org.uk/database, by entering the finds unique reference number, such as LIN-123456, into the search field.

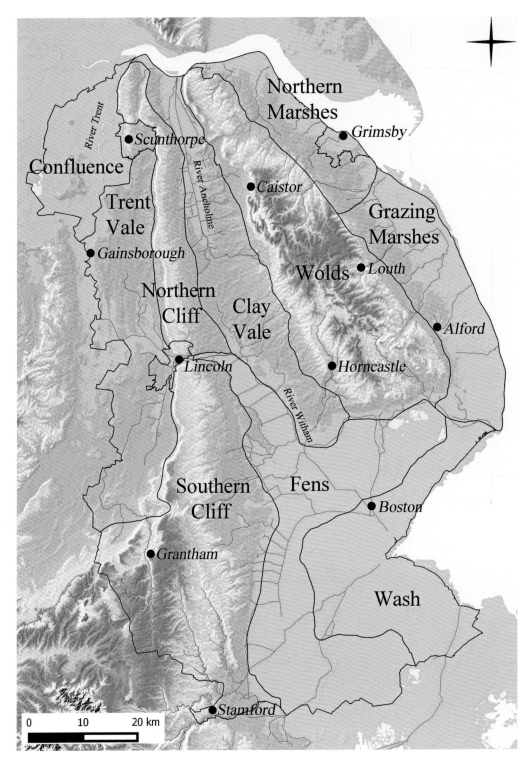

The landscape of Lincolnshire showing modern places. (Contains OS data © Crown Copyright and Land-Form Panorama data, 2015.)

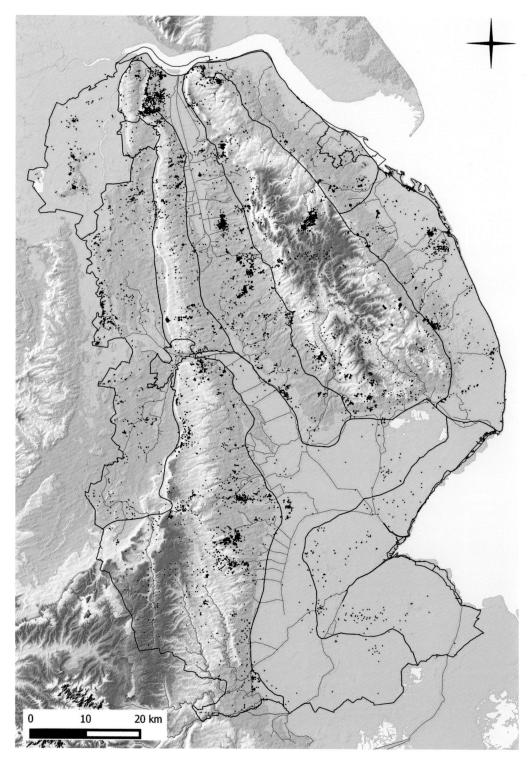

All finds from Lincolnshire reported to the Portable Antiquities Scheme (Contains OS data
© Crown Copyright and Land-Form Panorama data, 2015.)

Unlike many books on archaeology that have chapters divided chronologically, this one is arranged according to the different landscapes encountered in Lincolnshire. Lincolnshire boasts a diverse landscape, including coast, fen, upland limestone and chalk wold. The nature of these landscapes had a profound impact on how and where people could live and work. Many areas of the Fen and Coastal Marsh, for example, only became available after large-scale drainage works. By viewing finds in this way, we can begin to appreciate the different sorts of places where people settled in the past. Place, after all, is what makes us feel at home in both time and space.

Before turning to the fifty objects from the Portable Antiquities Scheme, we begin with a brief look at the history of archaeology in Lincolnshire, beginning in 1533 with the antiquarian John Leland.

Responsible metal detectorists are increasingly adding to our knowledge of the past through the accurate reporting of finds and sites, and also by assisting on archaeological excavations.

Newly discovered: a late medieval silver penny of Henry VIII, 'sovereign' type, emerges from the plough-soil near Louth.

Late Roman silver *siliqua* of Arcadius (383–408) found near Sleaford.

Introduction

In the southe ende of [Ancaster] be often tymes found in ploughing great square stones of old buildings and Romaine coyness of brasse and sylver. In the weste ende of it, were now medowes be, ar founde yn diching great vaultes.

(Hearne 1770: 29)

In 1533, the antiquarian John Leland was commissioned to embark upon a series of journeys across England and Wales to document the antiquities, topography and legends found across the regions. These journeys brought him into contact with many wonderful discoveries, such as those unearthed at the Roman settlement at Ancaster, Lincolnshire. Here he described the remains of Roman buildings, coins being found in the plough-soil, and also what appear to be stone-lined graves, found while digging ditches.

In the sixteenth century knowledge about the past was still rather hazy; antiquities were curiosities of a mysterious past, and the true depth of history represented by finds would still not be realised for several hundreds of years.

Leland's activities in recording discoveries marked an important turning point in archaeological recording. While he does not go into detail about precisely where these objects were found or exactly what the objects were, his work nonetheless demonstrated a growing awareness of the importance of noting down discoveries before they were lost. Further observations on Ancaster demonstrate the lure of antiquities:

At this end of the town, where a dove-cote stands, is Castle close, full of foundations appearing everywhere above ground: the ditch and rampire encompass it. Here are prodigious quantities of Roman coins found; many people in the town have traded in the sale of them these thirty years: they are found too in great plenty upon all the hills round the town, especially southward, and toward Castle-pits ... After a shower of rain the school-boys and shepherds look for them on the declivities, and never return empty.

(Stukeley 1776: 86)

These notes on Ancaster illuminate the great interest that people had about the past, and also the intimate understanding that they had about the local landscape. Stukeley describes children searching for Roman coins after a shower of rain – a practice that many field walkers searching for pottery, tile and flint still adhere to today. Many say that the best time to search for artefacts is after a shower of rain has made them more visible on the surface of a ploughed field. Such discoveries help to explain the occurrence of field names such as the 'money field'. Unfortunately we know nothing of the types of coins found by the schoolboys and shepherds, nor do we know where these artefacts are now.

The same is true of what is perhaps one of the most intriguing discoveries to have been unearthed in Lincolnshire, at Harlaxton in the early sixteenth century. Leland reports:

> An old Man of Ancaster told me ... that a Plough Man toke up in the Feldes of Harlaxton a two miles from Gratham a stone, under wich was a potte of Brasse, and a Helmet of Gold, sette with stones in it, the which was presented to Catarine Princes Dowager. There were Bedes of Silver in the Potte: and Writings corrupted.
>
> (Hearne 1770: 30)

We are told that this helmet was presented to Queen Katherine, first wife to Henry VIII. It has not been seen since. Quite what the discovery represents is a mystery, though some Roman parade helmets were made of gold and studded with jewels.

As time progressed, so too did the level of detail with which artefacts were recorded, discussed and collected by Lincolnshire antiquarians such as William Stukeley and Maurice Johnson. The latter was an influential barrister, fellow of the Society of Antiquaries of London and founder of the Spalding Gentlemen's Society in 1710, claimed to be the earliest provincial antiquarian society in England. The founding of the Spalding Gentlemen's Society marked an important turning point in the recording of antiquities in Lincolnshire. These early antiquarians were determined no longer to be 'strangers in their own land', as they called themselves; the recording of antiquities offered an important way of understanding their past.

Many of their enquiries into the past survive today in various minute books, letters, drawings and essays now held in the collections of the Spalding Gentlemen's Society. These show the society's founder, Maurice Johnson, as a tireless antiquary, diligently noting down and discussing all manner of discoveries.

William Stukeley described him as 'a most polite and universal scholar ... and a fluent orator and of eminence in his profession ... a lover of gardening, who had a fine collection of plants and an excellent cabinet of medals (coins)'. Many of these discoveries were recorded in their landscape context:

> Mr Samuel Brown of Lynn (but a native of Boston) told me since, in digging in his Fathers garden here, they found an urne full of ashes covered all over with lead. These things are sufficient proof that it is many centuries since the County of Holland in Lincolnshire was redeemed from the ocean, and I often conjecture that the road between Boston and Kirton being for the most part straight and broad, and all underlayd with Gravel, and in some places stone is a Roman work ...
>
> (Owen 1981: 7).

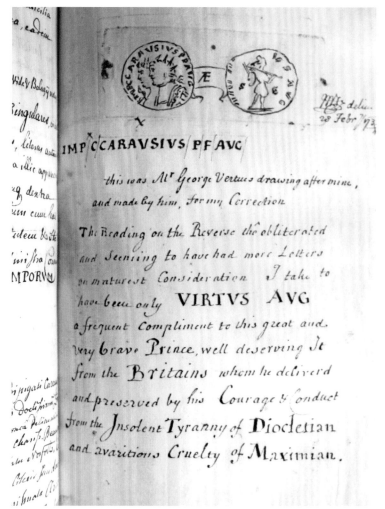

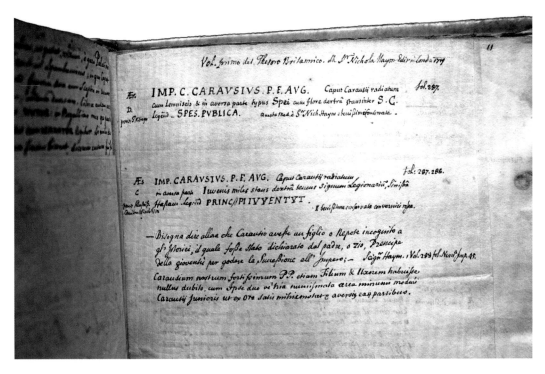

Section of a catalogue on the coins of Carausius, by Maurice Johnson. (Reproduced with the permission of the Spalding Gentlemen's Society)

Importantly, Johnson recognised that archaeological finds held a significance that extended far beyond them being curiosities. For example, Johnson's letters provide us with a fascinating insight into his religious and political beliefs, and show how he used artefacts to support various arguments and points of views. Johnson held a particular distaste for the Roman Empire, describing its rulers as a 'Series of Monstrous Men', while conversely showing great affection for 'British' heroes such as Boudica. To Johnson coins were evidence of political struggles between his forefathers, the 'Britons' as he calls them, and their oppressors, the Romans. Given Johnson's tendency to place coins within a religious or political narrative, it is possible that his views also reflected how England had to contend with the Continent, notably in the confrontation between Catholic European countries and Protestant England.

Over the next two hundred years, many outstanding discoveries would come to light as towns expanded and the rural landscape was worked more intensively. Some of the most spectacular were unearthed in the eighteenth and nineteenth centuries during works to the River Witham. These finds include prehistoric swords and spears, and also the famous Iron Age Witham shield, now in the British Museum. Most finds did not find their way into public ownership and unfortunately are now lost. Drawings survive of some of the more notable discoveries.

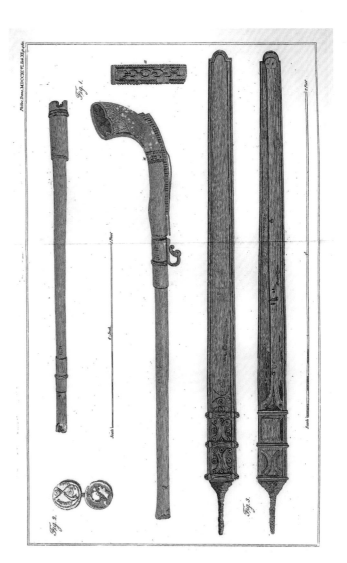

Among the many antiquities recovered from the River Witham is this Iron Age war trumpet (carnyx), found near Tattershall Ferry in 1768. An Iron Age copper-alloy scabbard with a sword of iron within it was found several years later in 1787 near the site of Bardney Abbey. Tragically, both items were melted down as part of a scientific experiment in 1796. (Drawing from Pearson 1796)

The recording of discoveries was, of course, a key activity of the City and County Museum in Lincoln when it opened in 1906. In addition to acquiring and exhibiting finds, curators used to attend farmers' markets to record the antiquities found by labourers working the land, and these finds were systematically recorded onto maps. All of this information is now recorded by Historic Environment Records (HERs), of which there are three in the region – in Lincoln, Scunthorpe and Grimsby. HERs are the most comprehensive source of information on the archaeology of an area and include not just historic finds, but also information on modern excavations, cropmarks, geophysical surveys and so on. PAS data form an important part of the evidence, but they can only be better understood in the light of the archaeological landscapes in which they have been found. The Lincoln Museum, now known as 'the Collection', continues to identify, acquire and exhibit finds today.

Left: One of the most exciting Roman finds to have been discovered in the county is this stone inscription to Mars, found by workmen digging a drain trench in Nettleham in 1961. The slab would have been set into an arch spanning the entrance to a temple enclosure. The stone is shown here being cleaned by the curator of the City and County Museum, Mr D. F. Petch.

Below: The inscription reads 'DEO MARTI RIGONEMETI ET NVMINIBVS AVGVSTORVM Q. NERAT. PROXSIMVS ARCVM DE SVO DONAVIT' ('To the god Mars, Lord of the Sacred Grove and to the Divinity of the Emperors, Quintus Neratius Proxsimus has given this arch from his own resources').

Chapter 1
Northern and Southern Cliff

A large 'tongue' of limestone extends north-east out of Leicestershire into Lincolnshire. Here it is known as the Southern Cliff – a major escarpment of Jurassic limestone, now dotted with attractive stone-built villages and imposing modern RAF bases. Dramatic views extend to the west from the cliff edge; to the east the limestone gently slopes to meet the Fen Edge. The escarpment tapers northwards to Lincoln where it is broken by the River Witham, and then on to the Humber. The Roman road known as Ermine Street runs along its spine. Buried remains of grand Roman villas and roadside towns lie dotted within this landscape.

Winter fields near Bitchfield. (Photograph by Alastair MacIntosh)

View from Belton Park to Grantham. (Photograph by Alastair MacIntosh)

The landscape that we see in Lincolnshire today is largely the result of a series of massive glacial events. Huge sheets of ice scoured the ground as the cold periods set in, and the large volumes of meltwater that resulted as the climate warmed again caused the formation and re-cutting of many major valleys. Because many of these events occurred after humans first occupied the region, most of the earliest axes found here are not at the places where they were originally dropped; rather, they were moved by high-energy water flows. As a consequence, most Palaeolithic axes are highly 'rolled', having a smooth, glossy appearance to them, such as can be seen on this example. It is impossible to date accurately, but was possibly used between 424,000 and 374,000 BC.

Most lower Palaeolithic axes in Lincolnshire have a glossy, 'rolled' appearance caused by water.

In spite of the wear, a strong raking light reveals ripples in the surface of the flint – crucial evidence of it having been knapped.

The distribution of palaeoliths shows a strong association with superficial deposits of glacial sands and gravels. Several examples were found during quarrying for aggregates at Whisby. The Whisby gravel pits have been converted to a nature reserve. (Copyright Dr John Esser. Reproduced by kind permission)

2. Stone phallic carving (LIN-CFA375)
Roman, late first to third century AD
Braceby. Length 392 mm

Not all finds reported to the PAS are discovered by metal detectorists. This elaborate stone carving was discovered among other stones in the back garden of a cottage near Braceby. The stone dates to the Roman period and shows an erect penis and a vagina. This motif was popular in Roman Britain and appears on variety of objects, from pendants to stone reliefs. It is probable that the stone was brought in from elsewhere, perhaps for use as a garden ornament. Notably, every phallic relief discovered in the East Midlands has been found in Lincolnshire.

Left: The phallus was a symbol of good luck as well as being a symbol of fertility and protection. The phallus was also thought to avert the evil eye, which may explain why it was commonly worn as an amulet. Amulets are also often associated with infant burials.

Right: Other images of fertility and reproduction include this Roman silver ring from Coningsby (LIN-336194). The intaglio depicts a male and female standing facing each other. The female, on the left, has her right arm raised and her hand cupping the male's head. The male is shown with an erect phallus and broad, muscular legs allowing him to be identified with the demi-god Pan or Faunus.

3. Copper-alloy knife handle (LIN-536F87)
Roman, first to fourth century AD
Barkston. Length 64 mm

The vast majority of myths, beliefs and local legends held by people in Roman Britain are now lost to us. As a consequence it is often difficult to fully understand the symbols and motifs seen on objects that clearly had some sort of religious or cult function. This knife handle depicts an erotic scene in which two adults and what appears to be a younger male are engaged in sexual activity. Only a handful of parallels are known, all of which generally show sexual intercourse between a man and a woman, with another crouched or flexed figure with his back to the woman. In this particular instance, the younger individual appears to be holding a severed head. It is likely that this represents a mythological scene.

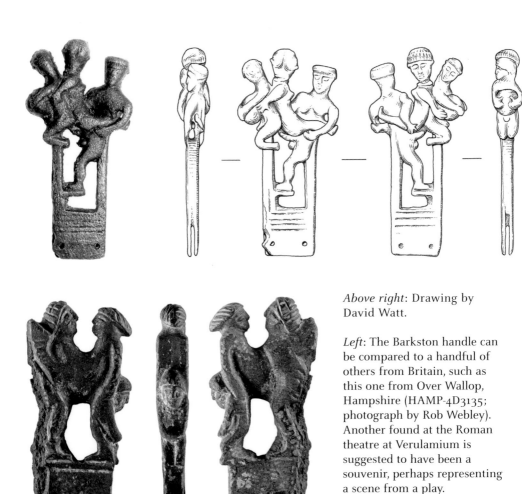

Above right: Drawing by David Watt.

Left: The Barkston handle can be compared to a handful of others from Britain, such as this one from Over Wallop, Hampshire (HAMP-4D3135; photograph by Rob Webley). Another found at the Roman theatre at Verulamium is suggested to have been a souvenir, perhaps representing a scene from a play.

4. Copper-alloy trumpet brooch (LIN-4CA644)
Roman, *c.* AD 43–100
Sleaford area. Length 75 mm

The period immediately prior to the Roman conquest has been described as a 'fibula event-horizon', owing to the flood of brooches that became available during this time. A startling number and variety of brooches were used in both urban and rural contexts after the conquest. Roman styles of brooches were frequently combined with insular art styles, which resulted in magnificent artefacts such as this trumpet brooch found near Sleaford. The head and foot of the brooch are decorated with cells of yellow, blue and orange enamel. In the centre is a large acanthus reel.

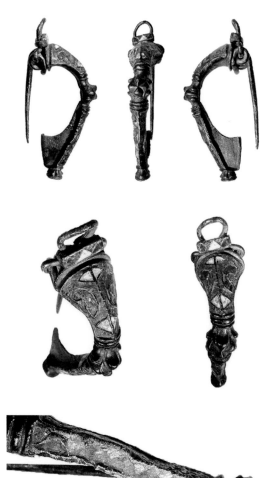

Trumpet brooches are common finds on Roman rural sites in Lincolnshire, but very few are decorated as elaborately as the Sleaford brooch. It was probably a bespoke item for a wealthy individual, rather than a mass-produced piece.

The decoration was achieved by cutting cells into the metal surface and then filling them with enamel.

The foot is decorated with a series of enamelled triangular and lozenge-shaped cells.

5. Copper-alloy finger from a statue (LIN-C6AFB3)
Roman, late first or early second century AD
Lincoln. Length 115 mm

Sculptures depicting humans are rarely seen before the Roman conquest in Britain. Bronze life-sized statues would therefore have been imposing figures and potent symbols of Roman power and authority. As such, statues were usually restricted to high-status private homes and public buildings in major towns. Owing to their high copper content, most statues were eventually melted down and made into other objects. Fragments of statues are, therefore, exceptionally rare. This finger was found close to a high-status Roman building on the outskirts of Lincoln. It was discovered 'eyes-only' while digging a post hole for a fence. We can't be sure who the statue represented, but the size of the finger indicates it was originally a life-sized representation. Fragments of an equestrian statue that may have once stood in the heart of Roman Lincoln have also been found in Lincoln and at North Carlton, close to the city.

Above: This object is the first finger from the right hand and appears to be making a formal gesture. This makes it almost certainly from a representation of an emperor. Could it be Domitian (AD81–96), under whom Lincoln was established as a colony for retired soldiers?

Left: The object is broken where the finger joins the rest of the hand. The interior of the thumb shows that it was actually made in two pieces welded together and smoothed over to form a continuous surface.

6. Copper-alloy spatula handle (LIN-F37090)
Roman, second or third century AD
Bourne. Length 51 mm

Gods and goddesses associated with particular crafts or activities were often depicted on associated artefacts in Roman Britain. This spatula handle found near Bourne dates to the second or early third century and is in the form of Minerva, the goddess of wisdom and learning. She is depicted wearing the *aegis*, a protective garment covering her shoulders and upper body, and with a gorgon's mask on the chest. Spatulas were used for smoothing down large areas of wax on writing tablets. They may have had a secondary use as votive items.

The base of the handle is split in order to secure an iron tang.

A similar spatula comes from the Roman settlement at Binbrook, Lincolnshire (NLM-9E4586).

7. Copper-alloy steelyard weight (LIN-1213A7)
Roman, first to fourth century AD
Sleaford area. Length 34 mm

The anticipation of what might be unearthed once a 'signal' has been located by metal detecting is often met with disappointment when a ring-pull or bit of aluminium foil emerges from the soil. In this instance the finder cleaned away the muck to reveal a rather grotesque face staring back at him. This Roman weight for a steelyard is in the form of the head of an adult male. He has a thin head, large nose and a large boil on the side of the forehead. One eyebrow is set higher than the other, making his face look out of proportion. He also has a large scar running down his right cheek. His mouth is shown slightly open, and his tongue drops motionless to one side. Only a handful of parallels are known from across the entire Roman Empire. Their significance is unclear.

Above: A large boil sits on the side of the head. The eye is filled with green enamel.

Left: Steelyard weights were hung from a straight-beam balance such as this one from South Staffordshire (WMID-184456). A second weight would have been attached to the left side of the arm.

8. Enamelled copper-alloy horse and rider brooches (LIN-A641C6, LIN-A5D8F7)
Roman, first or second century AD
Sleaford area. Lengths 33 mm, 34 mm

These two brooches were found together in the plough-soil and were presumably deposited at or around the same time. Both date to the late first or second century AD and are highly decorated in insular style. One shows an adult male riding a horse which gallops to the right. Both the rider and the horse have flowing hair, depicted by a series of lines. The other brooch shows a horse only, and has a body composed of cells of green and red enamel. It has been suggested that horse and rider brooches might represent a Romano-Celtic rider-god, or were perhaps emblems of a particular cult. Many examples have been found on temples in Britain. The accurate find spot reported by the finder means that we may be able to explore this site further in due course.

The abstract art represented on these brooches should not be seen as a poor attempt at a naturalistic scene. This form of representation is a very particular and well-executed form of insular art.

The decoration is formed by cutting out cells and then filling them with enamel.

A handful of other Roman horse and rider brooches are known from Lincolnshire. From top left to bottom right: Swinhope (NLM-A92AE9), Kirkby la Thorpe (LIN-F08CB4, LIN-B77EB6 and LIN-B75544) and Boston area (LIN-8A1366).

9. Copper-alloy knife handle (LIN-15BB58)
Roman, first to fourth century AD
Irnham. Length 55 mm

Some objects may have been used to tell stories as well as having been used for more mundane purposes. This Roman knife handle from Irnham, Lincolnshire, is a rare example on which a classical myth is depicted. The handle shows the mythical figures of Hercules and Antaeus having a wrestling match. Antaeus was a giant who challenged passers-by to wrestling matches. He challenged Hercules to a match, yet Antaeus kept on rejuvenating in strength every time Hercules threw him to the ground. Hercules eventually realised that the earth, Antaeus's mother, was the source of his opponent's strength. Accordingly, he held the giant aloft until all Antaeus's power had drained away. This final moment of victory is depicted on the handle; Hercules has his arms wrapped around Antaeus's waist, lifting him off the ground.

Left: Though worn, the outlines of the two wrestlers are still visible.

Right: Drawing by David Watt.

Below: Hercules is depicted on the reverse of this silver denarius of Trajan (BH-E7ED42). He stands on an altar, holding a club and a lion skin.

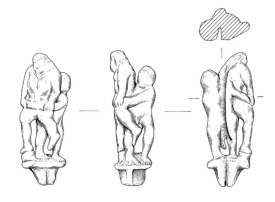

10. Cremation vessel (LIN-466281)
Roman, later first century AD
South Lincolnshire

Not all finds reported to the PAS are found by metal detectorists. In 2010 a member of the public was walking through a disused quarry when he spotted something eroding out of the side. On closer examination the object turned out to be a complete Roman urn containing the cremated remains of an adult, possibly a male. Two fragments of burnt animal bone were also found within the pot, which probably reflects the tradition of including food items on the cremation pyre during the funerary rite. This practice occurred most commonly within cremation deposits from the first century AD and usually included chickens, joints of beef, pork, mutton or goat and fish.

Right: An oval hollow in the quarry side shows where the pot was found.

Above: Cremated human bone emerges from the top of the vessel. These remains were later studied scientifically in controlled conditions.

11. Gilt copper-alloy florid cruciform brooch (LIN-1CE356)
Anglo-Saxon, sixth century AD
Folkingham. Length 173 mm

Deep ploughing has a detrimental impact on burials as well as settlements. Lincolnshire is rich in Anglo-Saxon burials of the sixth century – a period when objects were frequently placed in graves. This brooch is one object from a much larger assemblage that probably represents a plough-damaged cemetery. The excellent condition of the assemblage as a whole suggests that these artefacts had not been disturbed long before they were recovered from the plough-soil. This brooch, known as a florid cruciform brooch, is elaborately decorated with chip-carved motifs containing disjointed animals and masks carefully hidden within larger motifs. The brooch would have belonged to a high-status female.

Above right: Human faces and disjointed animals decorate the interior and perimeter elements of the brooch.

Below right: Included in the assemblage are two further brooches, one a great square-headed brooch (LIN-1DC8E5), and the other a cruciform brooch (LIN-1D8F47).

Below: This glass bead was found with the assemblage (LIN-1E5464). Necklaces comprising glass, ceramic and amber beads were popular in the sixth century. Many have been found accompanying burials.

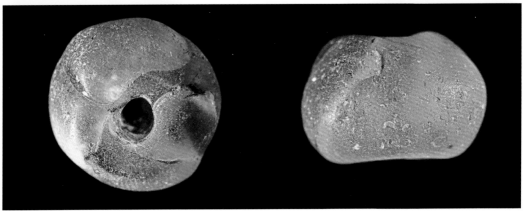

12. Gilt copper-alloy pendants (LIN-0ED385, LIN-D365D2)
Anglo-Saxon, late sixth to seventh century AD
Sleaford area. Diameter 29 mm, width 34 mm

These two pendants, or mounts, were found in the same field but were probably not deposited at the same time. The circular pendant is decorated with triple-stranded ornament and dates between AD 580 and 650. This object is similar to a mount attached to an iron bridle cheek-piece found at the royal burial site at Sutton Hoo, Suffolk. The crescent-shaped mount contains a cabochon-cut garnet – an addition popular in the second half of the seventh century. The terminals of the crescent are both in the form of a bird head with curved beak.

Right: The circular mount is decorated in 'Sahlin Style II' and comprises three stylised interlaced animals in profile.

Below left: The crescent-shaped mount comprises two birds opposing one another.

Below right: Close-up of the bird head showing small eye and curved beak.

13. Enamelled copper-alloy hanging bowl mount (LIN-89C232)
Anglo-Saxon, seventh century AD
Sleaford area. Diameter 50 mm

Hanging bowls are some of the most distinctive finds from Anglo-Saxon Lincolnshire. The Collection (Lincoln Museum) contains several examples, most of which have escutcheons decorated with so-called 'Celtic' art. Swirls, trumpet-spirals and triskeles form unending lines that occasionally discretely incorporate animals. Although used in the Anglo-Saxon period, these motifs are not the product of Angles or Saxons. Rather, they are thought to have been made in Northumbria, Scotland and the west of England. A digital reconstruction of this example found near Sleaford reveals three conjoined water birds.

Left: Reconstruction of the hanging bowl escutcheon showing repeating water birds and swirls.

Below left: Hanging bowls are high-status objects often found in graves, though an increasing number of escutcheons from these bowls is being recovered from the plough zone, where they derive from unknown contexts.

Below right: A similar escutcheon decorates the handle of this hanging bowl from Loveden Hill, Lincolnshire. (Image courtesy of The Collection: Art and Archaeology in Lincolnshire)

In 2012 a metal detectorist discovered an object covered with Anglo-Saxon runes. The inscription was studied by John Hines, who observes that the texts are remarkably close to a poem known as the *Azarias*. The text reads 'Let the glories of the created world and everything made, the heavens and the angels, and the pure water, [and all the power of creation upon Earth], bless Thee, kind Father'. The lines in turn represent a vernacular paraphrase of part of the Book of Daniel, 3:51ff, about the three youths in the fiery furnace. Hines suggests the inscription dates between AD 725 and 825.

The identification of this object is uncertain, though it was probably used in an ecclesiastical context. (Image courtesy of The Collection: Art and Archaeology in Lincolnshire)

Above: Close-up of the runic inscription using a microscope. (Images courtesy of The Collection: Art and Archaeology in Lincolnshire and Runes)

15. Gold finger ring (PAS-D077FE)
Late medieval to post-medieval, circa AD 1475–1525
Sleaford. Diameter 22 mm

Christianity was an important part of everyday life in medieval England. Artefacts often played a crucial role in this, not just as expressions of faith, but also as amulets that could protect the wearer from sickness and evil. This finger ring, called an iconographic ring due to the depiction of religious scenes, may have been used both as symbol and as amulet. The ring has five flat, oval panels on which are depicted the scenes of the *Annunciation*, the *Nativity*, the *Resurrection*, the *Assumption of the Virgin* and the *Ascension of the Lord*. The background to each scene is set with black enamel.

Gold ring showing the *Annunciation*, the *Nativity*, the *Resurrection*, the *Assumption of the Virgin* and the *Ascension of the Lord*. (Copyright of the trustees of the British Museum/Portable Antiquities Scheme)

Detail of the nativity scene. A figure kneels before the baby Jesus. An ox or donkey is shown in the background. While animals are a popular in depictions of the nativity, they are not actually mentioned in the gospels. (Copyright of the trustees of the British Museum/Portable Antiquities Scheme)

16. Hoard of gold Spanish-American doubloons (LIN-55BFE7)
Modern, buried after 1802
South-east Lincoln area. Diameter 37 mm

This hoard of gold Spanish-American doubloons is surely one of the most spectacular and exotic coin hoards ever to have been found in Lincolnshire. The hoard comprised eight coins, which might not sound a lot, but each example measures 37 mm in diameter and weighs close to 25 grams. These coins were minted in the late eighteenth and early nineteenth centuries at various sites in the Spanish South Americas, including what is now Columbia, Chile, Mexico and Bolivia. These regions contained rich deposits of gold and were mined intensively for bullion, making Spain one of the richest nations in the world. The denomination of each coin is the 'eight-escudos' – the highest denomination coin in circulation at the time. Its nickname, the 'doubloon', simply means 'to double' (available denominations were two, four, six, and eight escudos). Further research by the author established that the coins were actually remnants of a hoard of eighteen Spanish gold coins found in the early 1900s. Who buried them, and why they were never recovered, remains a mystery.

Top left: The obverses (heads) of the coins show Charles IV of Spain facing right, with the date below.

Top right: The reverses (tails) of the coins show the crowned arms of Spain within the collar of the Golden Fleece.

Above left: An eight escudos of Charles IV of Spain, struck in 1793 at Nuevo Reino (Bogota), Columbia.

Above right: To the left of the Golden Fleece is the mint mark (in this case S below O – for Santiago, Chile). To the right are the Assayer's initials.

17. Second World War German identity tag (LIN-CE1D45)
Modern, deposited 1945 to 1948
Wellingore. Width of tags 67 mm

The PAS does not usually record objects made after circa 1700, but exceptions are made for objects of local or national significance such as this German identity tag used during the Second World War. The dog tag is stamped with the owner's details, and reads 'Stamm komp J. E. B. 348' (Stammkompanie Infanterie-Ersatz-Bataillon 348). The upper part of the dog tag was normally buried with the soldier, while the lower was snapped off and sent back to the records office. Further research revealed that the soldier who owned this item returned to Germany in 1956. The tag was found near RAF Wellingore. At the end of the war the station was used as a camp for ex-prisoners of war from Germany, and remained in use to about 1948. Another German identity tag and an infantry badge were also found in the same area (LIN-75CDB6 and LIN-CE8D25).

Above left: The soldier's blood group 'O' is recorded on the bottom left of the upper tag, and to the right is his soldier number – sixteen.

Above right: A fragment of a second identity tag has been discovered in the same place. The top line reads '6664', which is the soldier's personnel number. The bottom line reads 'p Ld Schutz Ers Batl 13'. The letter 'p' at the far left next to the break would have been the last letter of the abbreviated word 'Komp[anie]', and so in full the inscription would have read 'Kompanie Landeschutz Ersatz Bataillon'.

Left: An incomplete German military badge from the Second World War. The badge depicts a rifle with strap within a wreath. An eagle is perched on the top of the wreath. This is an infantry assault badge and was awarded to German infantry soldiers who had participated in three campaigns.

Chapter 2
Confluence and Trent Vale

In the far north-west of the county the Isle of Axholme rises from the centre of a water world formed by the confluence of the Rivers Trent and Ouse. To the south the island is bounded by the River Idle, and to the west by the River Don. Scattered farmsteads dot a sinuous flat, low-lying landscape to the south following the River Trent. Alongside the Trent lie many of the county's most important riverside sites, such as Torksey, Marton and Gainsborough. The Northern Cliff rises dramatically to the east. The ancient routes of the Foss Dyke and Tillbridge Lane link the river to the cliff.

The Confluence. (Copyright Dr John Esser. Reproduced by kind permission)

The Julian Bower at Alkborough (north Lincolnshire), looking west over the Trent. (Copyright Dr John Esser. Reproduced by kind permission)

18. Hoard of gold staters (LIN-3400F2)
Iron Age, circa 50 BC
Saxilby area. Diameters 18–20 mm

Gold coins known as *staters* were being used in the East Midlands by the mid-first century BC. These coins show exquisite designs on both sides, revealing the competency of artists in late Iron Age Britain. These four coins were found very close together in a field near Saxilby and presumably once formed a hoard. The obverse (front) shows a laurel wreath and two crescents. This rather unusual design takes its influence from an ancient Greek coin of Phillip II of Macedon (382–336 BC), on the front of which is the head of Apollo. The Iron Age artists took the design and reinterpreted it according to local tastes. The reverse (back) shows a horse galloping left or right. Also found with the coins was a small pellet of gold weighing slightly less than a *stater*.

The majority of late Iron Age gold coins are found relatively unworn. This observation has led some to suggest that they were used for votive deposition rather than currency.

Two late Iron Age staters from the Stixwould hoard, photographed immediately after their discovery in 2008.

19. Copper-alloy vessel mount (LIN-D6E2B1)
Roman, early second century AD
Thonock. Length 67 mm

Animals as decorative motifs occur frequently on Romano-British artefacts, though this object is so far unique. The object is in the form of a three-dimensional fish, and was probably once attached to a vessel. Its scales are represented by four curving rows of crescent cells filled with green enamel. The gills and mouth are depicted in black enamel, while the eyes are depicted by a pellet of blue enamel surrounded by a ring of black enamel. The fish has a small dorsal fin on its back, and a lateral fin to either side at the base. The form of the fish suggests that it is a bottom-feeder.

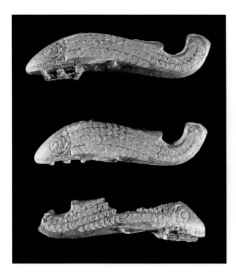

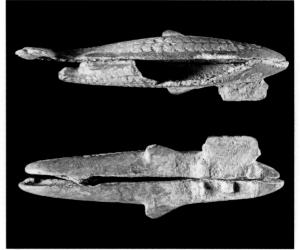

Above right: Top and bottom views of the fish.

Right: Drawing by David Williams.

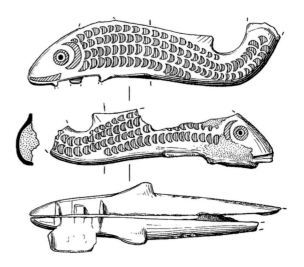

20. Copper-alloy captive figurine (DENO-EB7C77)
Roman, first to fourth century AD
Broxholme. Length 45 mm

At its maximum extent the Roman Empire stretched from North Africa to the southern parts of Scotland, and from the Atlantic to the Persian Gulf. Certain types of high-status gold and silver artefacts are almost ubiquitous across the Empire; others, such as this copper-alloy figurine of a captive or slave, have much more regional distributions. 'Captive' figurines have so far only been found on the Rhine/Danube frontier and in Britannia. The figure is of a young male, naked, and shown in a seated position with a rope bound round his neck, wrists and ankles. It is not known in what context these figurines were originally used.

Above: Incised images of bound captives are also seen on lead curse tablets, the captive representing the person being cursed. It is possible that the Broxholme figurine is associated with curses rather than being a representation of a slave.

Left: A rope binds the captive's neck, wrist and ankles.

21. Silver Islamic dirhams (NCL-544D22, DENO-708753)
Anglo-Saxon, first half of the tenth century AD
Revesby and Newton on Trent. Coin diameter 27 mm

Exotic artefacts are not uncommon in Lincolnshire given it has 80 km of coastland and a multitude of inlets and ports. One of the more unusual types of coin occasionally to be found in Lincolnshire is the Islamic dirham. Most are of the Abbasid or Samanid dynasties of the eighth to tenth centuries. These coins circulated in small numbers in Yorkshire and the East Midlands in the first half of the tenth century and are thought to have been brought over by Vikings. Most dirhams found in Lincolnshire are highly worn and often cut into smaller denominations. One particular example from the Newton-on-Trent area has been reworked into a hooked tag.

Above: A Samanid dirham dating to the reign of Amir Ahmad ibn Ismail (295–301 AH; AD 907–914), possibly dating to 300 AH (AD 912).

Right: A cut fragment of an Islamic dirham, probably of the Abbasid or Samanid dynasty, made into a hooked tag. Although a single coin does not normally constitute treasure, the secondary treatment means that this should be considered as an object rather than a coin, and thus as potential treasure.

Some 250 or so Russian lead seals have been found by metal detectorists in England. In Lincolnshire they are rare except for the area around Gainsborough. This is undoubtedly because of the important role that the port at Gainsborough played in the import of Russian flax and hemp in the late eighteenth and early nineteenth centuries. Ships bound for Gainsborough entered the Humber via Hull until the early nineteenth century, when Gainsborough was officially recognised as a port in its own right. The evidence for Anglo-Russian trade is preserved not just in the Hull Port Books, but also in the finds of lead seals that were once attached to the bales of flax and hemp. These seals provide information such as the name of the exporting port, the inspector's name, date and quality of the product. Crucially, they were discarded after use. The fifteen examples known to the PAS form a 'halo' around the town. Waste flax and hemp was collected and spread on nearby fields as manure; it might, therefore, be that these lead seals were accidently included with the waste. Equally, it might be that the seals represent dumping of waste from the town.

Bale seal for hemp, bearing the inspector's name I. M. Bushev, and the port name St Petersburg, dated 1834 (PAS ref. LIN-7BBEB5).

Bale seal displaying the heraldic arms of Narva, Estonia (PAS ref. LIN-68BA61).

46

Chapter 3
Clay Vale

Nestled between the Northern Cliff and the Wolds is the Clay Vale, a long stretch of low-lying land characterised for the most part by heavy clay soils. Rivers dominate this landscape; the Ancholme, Barlings Eau and many other smaller streams form a maze of waterways. In the south lie extensive areas of ancient limewoods. The Wolds rise to the east, often appearing as 'blackhills'.

The Clay Vale seen from the Wolds. (Copyright Dr John Esser. Reproduced by kind permission)

Kettleby Drain. (Copyright Dr John Esser. Reproduced by kind permission)

23. Copper-alloy bust of Antinous (LIN-B8FA27)
Roman, second century AD
Market Rasen area. Length 84 mm

Religion was an important part of everyday life in Roman Britain, a fact that is attested through the many portable artefacts discovered that depict or represent a deity. Mercury, Mars and Minerva are well represented in Lincolnshire. More rarely do we find images of demi-gods – persons who were deified after their death, such as the case near Market Rasen, where one high-status Roman site has produced what might be one the finest bronzes to have been found in Lincolnshire. This mount, which probably once attached to a tripod for a bowl, depicts Antinous, the Emperor Hadrian's alleged homosexual lover.

Left: Antinous drowned in the River Nile. Such was Hadrian's grief that he founded an entire city to him in Egypt, called Antinopolis.

Middle: Many statues depicting Antinous have been found at Antinopolis. All show the same features – wavy hair, broad neck and shoulders, muscular body and small breasts.

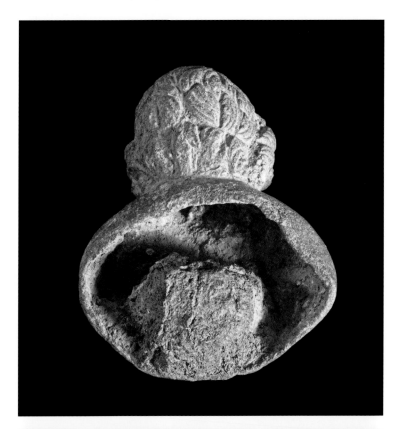

An iron shank
protrudes from the
reverse of the mount.

Detail of the top of
the head.

24. Assemblage of copper-alloy coins (SWYOR-834D8D)
Roman, first to fourth century AD
Lincoln area. Diameters between 14 mm and 28 mm

Context is everything to an archaeologist; the sealed layers in which an object is found can give vital clues to dating or circumstance of deposition, and can reveal any associated finds. Deep ploughing can destroy these layers, bringing many years of history into one single context: the plough zone. This can make it very difficult to know what finds were buried at the same time. In 2014 a metal detectorist searching fields near Lincoln discovered 111 Roman coins in the same area. At first these looked like a hoard that had been dispersed by the plough, but closer analysis of the dates of the coins revealed they could not have been buried together at the same time. Rather, they were simply the accumulation of losses over four centuries of occupation.

Below: *Nummus* of Constantine I. This coin is commonly found on rural settlements in the region.

25. Tinned copper-alloy mirror (LIN-0B4401)
Roman, third century
Linwood. Diameter 120 mm

In spite of over 75,000 finds having been reported in Lincolnshire, this Roman mirror is unique in Britain. Found near Linwood in 2015, it is one of the most enigmatic objects to have been brought in for recording. The mirror dates to the third century and was probably made in Trier or Cologne. It is decorated with concentric circles on the back, while the front is slightly convex. Both sides were originally tinned and then highly polished to create a reflective surface. Microscopic analysis of the convex side shows a series of very fine polishing marks. When found in graves on the Continent, they usually accompany high-status females who were also buried with other elaborate objects that suggest an official or military connection.

Left: Mirrors are more often found on military and urban sites than rural sites. This example appears to have come from a high-status rural settlement.

Below left: Dark patches of tinning survive on the surface of the mirror.

Below right: Microscopic analysis of the surface reveals fine polishing marks. (Image courtesy of Siemens, Lincoln)

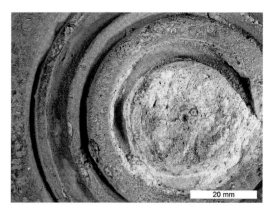

26. Gold cross-pendant (LIN-75FD54)
Anglo-Saxon, seventh century AD
Newball. Length 40 mm

The Newball cross was discovered in 2005 and remains one of the most unusual pieces of goldwork to have been found in the county. The cross is thought to be a direct reference to Christianity, which would accord well with the seventh-century date given to the object. The front has a small opening, also in the shape of a crucifix. Quite whether this once contained a fragment of a relic or perhaps a gemstone is unclear. Interestingly, the crucifix shape of the pendant is upside down when suspended from a necklace. This would be entirely appropriate if it was used as personal amulet, since it would be the correct way round when viewed by the wearer.

The hollow inset suggests this may have once held a relic.

27. Silver coin hoard (LIN-747367)
Medieval, buried circa 1320–1333 AD
Apley. Diameters circa 18 mm

The discovery of a hoard always raises questions that are often difficult to answer. Why was it buried? Who owned it? Why was it not recovered? The Apley hoard contains 146 silver pennies, most of which were issued by Edward I (1272–1307) and Edward II (1307–1327). The majority of coins were struck at various mints across England, while two were struck in Ireland. Two further pennies were issued by the King of Scotland, Alexander III (1280–1286), while one coin was an imitation of a penny of Arnold, Count of Looz. Owing to the lack of coins dating between 1320 and 1333, which were circulating in large numbers at the time, the hoard was probably deposited in the period c. 1317–1320.

This hoard was found by a gentleman who had only been out a few times with his metal detector. Few are so lucky; most never find anything quite so spectacular, even after years of searching.

Almost all the coins are in good condition and show little or no signs of having been clipped; this suggests the hoarder was carefully selecting the best coins for burial.

28. Copper-alloy mace head (LIN-871975)
Medieval, thirteenth century AD
Fiskerton. Diameter 58 mm

Medieval mace heads are rare finds in Britain. Fewer than forty examples are known, around half of which have been recorded through the PAS. These are rather crude, heavy items, being made of leaded bronze and usually having three rows of pyramidal or semi-pyramidal knops. Quite often these knops are down-turned – evidence for them having been used before deposition. However, several clues suggest they were not used in battle. First, the socket is too small to have allowed it to be swung with any force without breaking the wooden shaft. Second, many of the more elaborate examples found in Ireland are highly decorated, with some also having openwork shafts. When found in context, or seen on sculpture, this form of mace appears to have ecclesiastical associations. It may be the case that these are ceremonial maces rather than weapons.

Above left: Knopped mace heads are distinctively different from Norman mace heads, being a type that originated in Kiev in the ninth century, and which appears to have been introduced to Britain from Scandinavia in the thirteenth century.

Above middle: Traces of the wooden shaft survive in the socket. With a diameter of just 17 mm, the shaft would have easily broken if used with any force.

Above right: Drawing by David Watt.

Right: Distribution of medieval knopped mace heads in England and Wales.

29. Lead pilgrim badge (LIN-D80A35)
Medieval, thirteenth to mid-fourteenth century AD
Wragby. Length 30 mm

Pilgrimage was an important part of life in medieval England, and individuals were expected to make at least one major journey to a shrine in their lifetime. Market stalls often lined the entrances to shrines, and here one could buy a variety of souvenirs such as badges and small vessels known as *ampullae*. This badge is in the form of Thomas Becket and is one of a well-known series of badges that are miniature copies of the fourteenth-century, life-sized, mitred-bust reliquary of St Thomas in Canterbury Cathedral. The badge would have been worn on the hat or on the outer clothing and would have been used as an amulet. The supposed miracle-working powers of reliquaries were thought to transfer onto the objects copied from them, hence the popularity of pilgrim badges.

Left: Lead is a very soft metal and does not survive well in the plough-soil. The majority of pilgrim badges are found incomplete.

Below: Other forms of badges associated with St Thomas Becket are known. This example from Branston is in the form of a miniature ship, probably the type known as a hulc. It is likely that this souvenir is a Canterbury product, made to represent the ship that carried St Thomas Becket across the Channel to Sandwich.

30. Gilt copper-alloy cross mount (LIN-A7A7E7)
Medieval, late twelfth or thirteenth century AD
Legsby. Length 114 mm

The image of the crucified or suffering Christ was popular in medieval England. This mount dates to the thirteenth century and would have been attached to a processional cross or perhaps an altar. Christ is shown crucified, wearing a crown and robes. His head is angled slightly down to his right, and his face has a sorrowful expression. Although the mount is worn, details of the ribs are visible; his body slumps forwards. His lower legs merge towards the feet, now missing, where they were nailed to the cross. The surface of the metal has been gilded and inset with enamel.

The mount is made from very thin metal. It is unlikely that this object would have survived for long in the plough-soil.

31. Copper-alloy padlock (LIN-80D373)
Post-medieval, circa 1550–1650 AD
Hatton. Length 32 mm

One of the more unusual finds to have been reported to the PAS is this combination padlock, dating from around 1550 to 1650. The padlock has five rotating discs held between two fixed outer discs. All but one of the central rotating discs have five symbols stamped on them, the other only having four, although the fifth may be completely worn away. Curiously the outer discs only have two and one symbol respectively, and these are not in alignment with one another. Accordingly, the opening combination must have consisted either of all seven symbols in diagonal line, or of five or six symbols in a straight line. A similar example from Suffolk was decorated with letters, not symbols, and may have opened with the combination 'open'. Another, now in the British Museum, opened with the word MARCI.

Far left: This is the only example of a combination padlock to have been recorded in Lincolnshire since the scheme began in 2003. Only eight have been recorded nationally.

Left: X-Radiography of the padlock reveals its internal components.

Below left: Schematic plan of the symbols. (Drawing by David Watt)

Below: Drawing by David Watt.

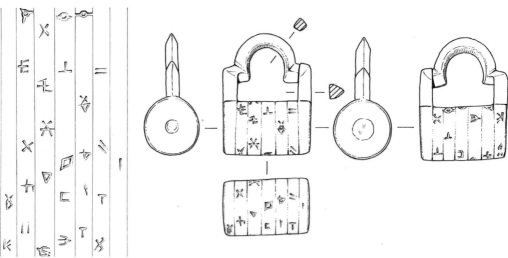

Chapter 4
Wolds

Rolling chalk hills and hidden valleys formed by glacial action and meltwater give way to vast open skies. This is a land of farmsteads, picturesque villages, good pubs and pleasant walks along both ancient and modern paths.

The Wolds, near Croxby. (Copyright Dr John Esser. Reproduced by kind permission)

The Wolds, near Wold Newton. (Copyright Dr John Esser. Reproduced by kind permission)

32. Copper-alloy miniature objects (e.g. LIN-9DE863)
Roman, first or second century AD
Nettleton. Various sizes up to 60 mm

Close to the highest point on the Lincolnshire Wolds lies a magnificent Romano-British settlement. The site, which commands extensive views to the west, has also produced some of the most remarkable miniature objects known from Britain. The assemblage includes over thirty shields, spears, swords and axes, all shrunk down into miniature form. It is almost certain that these items represent offerings made at a temple or shrine. Several of the shields have small holes in them where they were probably hammered to a door or wooden post.

A selection of the twenty-two miniature shields found at Nettleton. Single finds are infrequently discovered in Britain, and only one other hoard, from Salisbury in Wiltshire, has produced similar quantities. The Salisbury hoard contained twenty-four miniature shields, forty-six miniature cauldrons and two miniature axes.

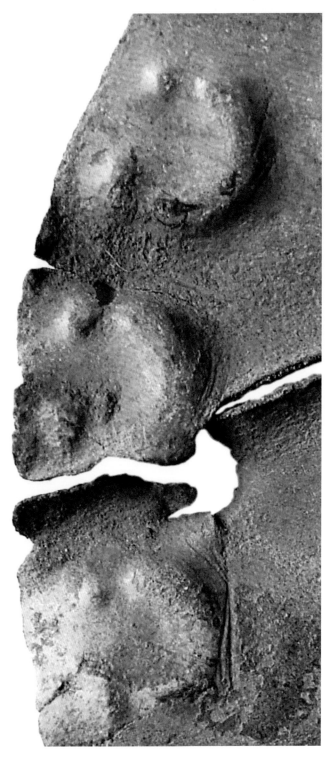

One of the shields is decorated with crescent motifs. Dr Julia Farley has suggested these might represent fittings or mouldings seen on full-sized Iron Age shields.

In the early and middle Iron Age full-sized weapons were deposited in the River Witham as high-status votive offerings. The Nettleton Top material appears to continue this tradition in miniature form, perhaps in some cases intentionally imitating the style of earlier artefacts such as the famous Witham Shield of middle Iron Age date.

A selection of the swords, spears and axes.

The Church of St John the Baptist at Nettleton dominates the foreground. The settlement of Caistor rises in the background. (Copyright Dr John Esser. Reproduced by kind permission)

33. Copper-alloy vessel mount (LIN-40CE20)
Roman, first to third century AD
Winceby. Length 37 mm

Animals appear frequently on late Iron Age and Romano-British artefacts. Many appear to have held religious or ritual significance, such as the boar, which is also frequently depicted on late Iron Age coins produced in the East Midlands. Vessel mounts also frequently take the form of animals, especially bulls. This example shows a bull in a rather abstract style; the horns are overemphasised, and the eyes are shown by pointed oval cells. The front hooves of the animal emerge below the head on either side of the point where the mount was riveted to the bowl. The bowl is likely to have been used for ritual purposes.

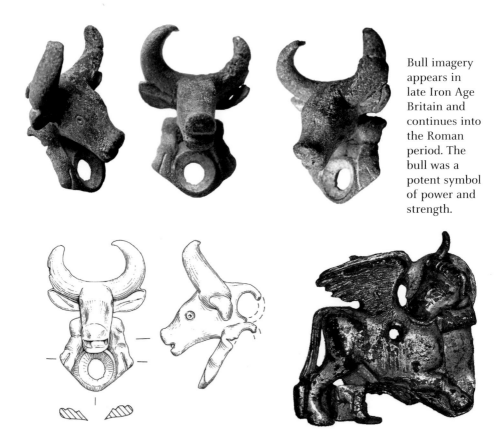

Bull imagery appears in late Iron Age Britain and continues into the Roman period. The bull was a potent symbol of power and strength.

Above left: Drawing by David Watt.

Above right: The image of the bull took on a different meaning centuries later. In Christian iconography the bull symbolised St Luke, the evangelist. This medieval mount from Pinchbeck, dating to the fourteenth or fifteenth century, shows a winged bull standing over a scroll (NLM169). The mount was probably once fixed to a crucifix.

34. Copper-alloy figurine of Mercury (LIN-25CC02)
Roman, first to third century AD
Nettleton. Length 81 mm

Romano-British settlements are dotted along the western edge of the Wolds, especially in the area between Ludford and Caistor, roughly following the line of the Roman road known as Caistor High Street. Most homes would have contained a small shrine at which offerings and prayers could be made, and it is possible that this was the original context of this figurine of Mercury. The deity stands naked except for a *paenula* (cloak) draped over the left shoulder and left arm. He has curly hair and wears a cap with two wings – a distinctive feature of Mercury. In his right hand he holds a money bag, a symbol which attests to his role as the god of trade and commerce.

Above: Figurines such as this one of Mercury may have been kept in small household shrines used for private worship.

Right: Mercury was the messenger of the gods. The wings on the cap allowed him to travel quickly.

Other probable shrine figurines from Lincolnshire include these two eagles found near Sleaford (LIN-383C86 and LIN-7645F7). In Roman mythology eagles were often associated with Jupiter.

Although the Roman sun god Sol is frequently seen on coins, this figurine found near Sleaford is the only example recorded by the PAS (LIN-A65125).

35. Gold finger ring (LIN-22EEF2)
Roman, first to third century AD
Nettleton. Diameter 25 mm

The same site that produced the miniature objects has also produced one gold and several silver finger rings that display the image of Vulcan, the smith god. Here he is depicted holding a pair of tongs in one hand, and a hammer over an anvil in the other. The concentration of Vulcan imagery at Nettleton might be related to the natural outcrops of ironstone in this part of the county. Iron was an important resource in Roman Britain, and these rings may, therefore, indicate worship of the deity at the very place where the source of iron is exposed.

The close relationship that these Vulcan rings have with the landscape highlights the importance of accurately recording where objects were found.

36. Roman silver TOT ring (e.g. LIN-944EE5)
Roman, second or third century AD
Various sites in Lincolnshire

Until recently, the Celtic god Toutatis was relatively unknown in Britain; only a handful of objects testified to the deity, who was often paired with the Roman god Mars. This has changed largely because of evidence now provided by an enigmatic series of finger rings in copper-alloy, silver and gold bearing the inscription TOT – an abbreviation of the god name. These rings date to the late second or third centuries and carry a variety of decorative motifs and abbreviations. Over 100 examples are now known, but curiously nearly all of them have been found in the East Midlands, especially in Lincolnshire, in what was probably the Roman administrative *civitas* of the Corieltavi. The name Toutatis is thought to mean 'protector of the tribe', and given the strong association with the Corieltavi it is interesting to speculate whether these rings indicate a tribal devotion.

Above left: A selection of TOT rings.

Above right: The most complete inscription on a TOT ring comes, ironically, from a site far away from the main concentration – at Hockliffe in Bedfordshire (BH-C3A8E7). One shoulder is missing, but the inscription as a whole would have read DEO TOTA VTERE FELIX (to the god Totatis, use this happily).

Left: The systematic recording of portable antiquities across the country has allowed several regional trends to emerge, such as the concentration of TOT rings in the East Midlands, especially in Lincolnshire. The black line indicates the hypothesised *civitas* of the Corieltavi.

It is a strange paradox that although there are many Scandinavian place names in Lincolnshire, there are very few objects that can be directly related to the Vikings. One of the few exceptions is this exquisite gold pendant in the form of Thor's hammer, Mjollnir. Thor was one of the principal deities of the Vikings and is often associated with war. The pendant is decorated with small, punched quatrefoils, or perhaps miniature hammers. The majority of English-made Thor's hammer pendants are made of silver and are undecorated, while those from Scandinavia are usually highly decorated and often in gold.

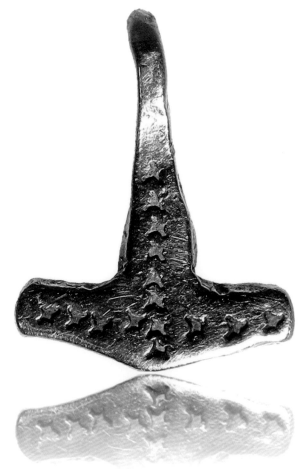

Mjollnir is the hammer of Thor, the Norse god of thunder. These pendants would have been potent symbols of paganism in what was largely a Christian landscape. A silver hammer pendant is also known from the Viking winter camp at Torksey (DENO-BD00C3).

The Venetians were important traders in late medieval Europe. Venetian galleys habitually set out for England and Flanders during May and stayed until late August or early September. From the ports of London, Sandwich and later Southampton, they sold various exotic goods, including pepper, cloth and glass. They also bought large quantities of wool, a commodity which was particularly well sourced on the Lincolnshire Wolds. The galleys also brought with them large quantities of Venetian silver *soldini*. These coins plugged a gap resulting from the shortage of English halfpennies. They circulated illegally and extensively until the government made several attempts to stamp them out.

Soldino of the first incursion struck under Doge Michael Steno (1400–13). The obverse (front) shows the Doge holding a banner. The reverse shows the lion of St Mark holding the book of the gospels.

Soldino of the second incursion struck under Doge Leonardo Loredan (1501–1521). The obverse (front) shows the Doge kneeling, receiving a banner from St Mark. The reverse shows Christ standing, holding a cross.

Soldini were sometimes converted into jewellery. This *soldino* of Doge Leonardo Loredan, found in Staffordshire, has been made into a button (WMID-F4E937).

39. Gold pendant (DENO-65C775)
Medieval, fifteenth century AD
Horncastle area. Length 21 mm

The question as to whether a find represents an unfortunate casual loss, intentional concealment, or something else is often difficult to establish. Such is the case with this stunning pendant, which dates to the fifteenth century. The pendant has an elaborate circular frame made from twisted wire. The centre of the pendant contains a large amethyst set in a gold frame, from which extend a series of 'rays'. Three gold chains fall eloquently from the base of the pendant. The pendant as a whole appears to represent the sun, a symbol adopted by Yorkists during the Wars of the Roses.

A similar pendant was found in the Fishpool hoard. The hoard was found in 1966 in Ravenshead, Nottinghamshire, and contained 1,237 gold coins, in addition to gold jewellery.

On 18 November 1800, Ordery (Audrey) Appleyard, aged twenty-three, was transported to Australia on the *Earl Cornwallis*, having been convicted at Lincoln of stealing. She arrived in Port Jackson, New South Wales, 206 days later, on 12 June 1801 along with 296 other convicts. Just ninety-five convicts were female, of whom eight died during the voyage. Appleyard was sentenced to seven years, but she made a new life for herself, marrying John Gowen in 1805. Gowen was one of the earliest settlers of Australia. Ordery died on 17 October 1819 aged 42, mother to five children. This 'convict love token' was apparently made by Ordery for her mother, just before she saw her for what appears to have been the last time. One side of the token reads 'Ordery Appleyard 1800'. The other side reads 'Mother my trust is in God and I will not fear what man can do unto me.' So-called 'convict love tokens' were frequently made by convicts as a way of leaving a memento behind for their loved ones.

The Earl Cornwallis, circa 1790, by Thomas Daniell, 1749–1840. Grey ink and grey wash over graphite on medium, smooth, cream laid paper. (Yale Center for British Art, Paul Mellon Collection)

Chapter 5
Grazing and Northern Marshes

Salt marsh and dunes give way to ancient enclosure and modern fields. 'Look for the bumps,' say most finders. Here gentle mounds rise from an otherwise flat landscape; nearly all contain the remains of medieval occupation. In the north, industrial complexes rise from an otherwise flat and wet landscape. Networks of ditches hint at post-medieval drainage, as land was fought from water.

The Northern Marshes. The Humber Bridge rises in the background. (Copyright Dr John Esser. Reproduced by kind permission)

The Coastal Grazing Marsh seen from Anderby. The Wolds rise in the background.

The torc is one of the most iconic objects from Bronze Age and Iron Age Britain. However, very few from either period have been found in Lincolnshire in comparison to Norfolk. This example from the Grimsby area dates to the middle Bronze Age and can be compared to a series of cast torcs from Ireland. The frame has a spiral decoration made by casting rather than twisting. The surface has a number of areas that indicate the torc was broken up by heating immediately before deposition. Quite whether this was done for recycling or for ritual purposes is unclear.

The torc has the appearance of being twisted, but it was in fact cast.

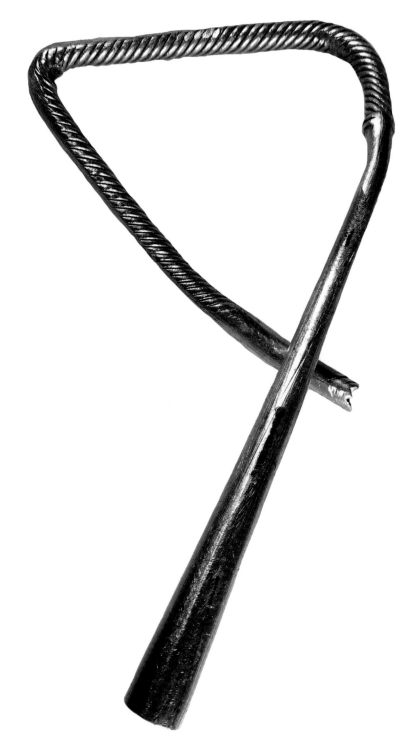

Non-destructive X-ray fluorescence analysis undertaken by the Department of Conservation and Scientific Research at the British Museum indicated a surface composition of approximately 75–77 per cent gold, 16–18 per cent silver, the rest being copper.

42. Gold and garnet necklace (LIN-18EEC1)
Anglo-Saxon, seventh century AD
Alford area. Length of pendant 19 mm

In spite of the potential for later inundations to bury archaeological deposits, a surprising number of high-status objects dating to the late sixth or seventh centuries have been found in the Grazing Marshes. In all cases, these come from shallow rises in the landscape, away from seasonal floods. In 2011 four items that presumably came from a single high-status gold necklace were found in the plough-soil. The assemblage includes two spacers, one back-plate from a pendant, and one gold and garnet pendant. The spacers and the pendant are decorated with exquisite filigree beading, while the pendant itself contains a cabochon-cut garnet. Similar necklaces have been found in graves of high-status women elsewhere in England, such as at Sheffield's Hill near Roxby, Lincolnshire.

Top: The style of decoration seen on the gold spacers is known as filigree, which refers to the technique of soldering tiny beads or wire to the surface of an object.

Above right: Filigree is commonly seen on gold-work of the seventh century. This pendant found near Skegness displays intricate swirls of gold beading (LIN-7A7C04).

43. Glass setting (LIN-252D32)
Anglo-Saxon, eighth or ninth century
Louth area. Diameter 35 mm

'Eyes-only' finds can be just as spectacular as those found using a metal detector. This Anglo-Saxon glass setting was discovered sitting on top of the plough-soil after a shower of rain. The body is made of dark purple/black coloured glass, and the domed surface is decorated with seven lines of twisted coloured glass radiating from the centre. The back and sides of the mount are rough, suggesting that it was originally set into a casing, possibly on a hanging bowl. Parallels suggest a date between the second half of the eighth and the ninth century.

The presence of glass on middle Saxon sites usually indicates high-status activity.

44. Stone carving (LIN-D29333)
Medieval, thirteenth or fourteenth century AD
Saltfleetby St Peters. Length 250 mm

This limestone head is certainly one of the more unusual objects to have been reported to the PAS. The head dates to the thirteenth or fourteenth century and was used as a label stop or corbel. Similar stops can still be seen in medieval churches today, many of which depict angels, saints, or in some cases the benefactors of the church. In this instance the head is that of a young-looking male, probably an adolescent. This stop was found in a ploughed field near to the site of the former church of Saltfleetby St Peters, from which it presumably originated. The limestone is only slightly weathered, suggesting that it was originally located inside the church or within the porch.

Carved human heads are often thought to have been based on local faces.

45. Lead spindle whorl (LIN-D92A22)
Late Saxon or medieval, eleventh century AD
Saltfleetby. Diameter 26 mm

Medieval spindle whorls often carry elaborate moulded or incised decoration, and at times these are mistaken for writing. This rare example from Saltfleetby, close to the coast, is the real thing. Dating to the eleventh century, this example is covered in runes in addition to a stylised plant motif on the top. The inscription is unclear in parts, but John Hines has suggested it reads 'Óðinn and Heimdallr and Þjálfa, they ... help thee Úlfljótr and...' The inscription appears to be a prayer invoking two gods of the major pre-Christian Viking pantheon. These prayers may have been chanted as prayers of protection into the very fabric of the garments as they were being made. This find is important evidence for the use of Old Norse in a North Sea coastal community in the early eleventh century.

The text begins on the vertical wall and reads 'Óðinn and Heimdallr and Þjálfa, they...'

Above: The text on the flat base reads '… help thee Úlfljótr and …'

Below: A number of havens, now silted up, used to provide access to Saltfleetby St Clements. Saltfleet Haven, to the north of Saltfleetby St Clements, is still in use today. (Photograph by Alastair MacIntosh)

46. Lead pilgrim badge (LIN-FD4722)
Medieval, thirteenth to fifteenth century AD
Hogsthorpe. Diameter 26 mm

One of the most intriguing trends to have emerged from PAS data is the concentration in East Lindsey of medieval badges dedicated to St Margaret of Antioch. These distinctive badges or pendants show St Margaret holding a cross in her right hand and a book in her left, and standing on a dragon. This relates to the story of St Margaret, who was reputed to have been swallowed by Satan in the form of a dragon. She escaped when her cross irritated the dragon's innards, causing him to vomit his ill-gotten meal. The reverse reads IHS – probably an abbreviation of 'Iesus Hominum Salvator' (Jesus, saviour of Men). These badges are thought to be associated with the cult centre at the church of St Margaret in Ketsby, Lincolnshire.

Left: Digital cutting out of the St Margaret and Dragon motif enhances the detail of the scene.

82

Chapter 6
Fens and Wash

Before large-scale drainage, the Fens and the Wash were dynamic landscapes formed of rivers, pools and seasonally inundated land, all of which could change over a short period of time. Historic settlements hug the silt banks of ancient creeks; earlier occupation lies hidden deep below sediment. The sky weighs heavily on the landscape. Venture further into the Wash and one encounters a series of earthen banks which mark the extent of former coastlines. Prairie-style fields dominate a landscape cut by the inlet to the medieval port of Boston, the sway of ships now replaced by articulated lorries.

Winter fields, viewed from the bridge over the River Welland outside the Old Coach House in Market Deeping. (Photograph by Alastair MacIntosh)

A lane, raised from the surrounding landscape, runs along the Fen Edge near Bourne. (Photograph by Alastair MacIntosh)

The collapse of Roman rule in Britain brought with it the almost total cessation in the use of coins for the next 200 years or so. Coins reappear in Lincolnshire first with gold examples brought in from the continent around 630, followed by a large influx of silver coinage towards the end of the century. The early gold coins are rare in Lincolnshire, but one site thought to be a market associated with the Anglo-Saxon centre at Sleaford has produced two examples. Both date from between 630 and 640 and were struck in Frisia. The obverse bears the motif of a double cross, formed of a single vertical stroke with two crossing bars.

Only a handful of these unusual coins are known in England. The type originated in Friesland, but some might be English copies.

The granulated reverse seen on these coins is puzzling.

By the end of the seventh century, silver coins known as *sceattas* were circulating widely across the East Midlands. This example was found near Louth (LIN-13F9D2).

Many objects were used for several different purposes over their life, taking on new meanings over time. The papal *bulla* is such an item. Papal *bullae* are seals, made of lead, which were used to authenticate official documents sent out by Rome. One side usually depicts the faces of St Peter and St Paul, accompanied by the abbreviations SPA (St Paul) SPE (St Peter) above, which identifies them as such. The other side gives the name of the pope in office at the time. This example from Long Sutton was issued under Pope Alexander III (1159–1181). *Bullae* were often reused as amulets; some have been found accompanying burials. This example has been pierced, presumably for use as a pendant.

The depictions of St Paul and St Peter are very distinctive, as can be seen more clearly in this example from Wiltshire (WILT-5D31FF). Paul has straight hair and beard, while Peter has curly hair and a short beard represented by pellets.

87

49. Copper-alloy knife handle (LIN-F16D33)
Post-medieval, seventeenth century
Fishtoft. Length 71 mm

From the watery landscape of the Fens comes this object with a watery tale. This knife handle dates to the seventeenth century and depicts a scene from the Biblical book of Jonah. Jonah was called by God to go and preach to the citizens of Nineveh, but he disobeyed and instead fled to Tarshish. He boarded a ship at Joppa and set sail, but during his journey a mighty storm arose. Fearing that the storm was the result of God's anger, the sailors threw Jonah overboard where he was then swallowed by a large fish. He spent three days praying in the belly of the fish, after which he was spat out. The knife handle shows the moment Jonah emerged from the mouth of the fish.

The Book of Jonah was probably written in the late fifth to early fourth century BC.

A clearer example reported to the PAS was found at Barley, Hertfordshire (BH-8D8C03).

The majority of artefacts discovered in the soil cannot be traced back to a named individual. Where this is possible it often makes the artefact quite poignant. This medal is testimony to an initiative undertaken in the 1780s and '90s to help poor children across some 143 parishes in Lincolnshire. It was issued by the Society for the Promotion of Industry, who set up places where poor children were taught to knit before they were six, and to spin before they were nine years of age. Materials were provided by the society, and children were paid 5*d* a day. Medals and other rewards such as stockings and hats were given to the best weavers and spinners each year. This particular medal was given to Sam Wright, aged ten.

Enhanced view of the inscription, which reads '5 Premium, Sam Wright, Aged 10, [178]'.

Final thoughts

The Portable Antiquities Scheme has been a huge success, and the addition of 75,000 new finds from Lincolnshire is certainly something to celebrate. This book has charted some of the most interesting finds reported so far, and has explored a range of themes from art to object biographies. However, archaeological finds are much more than objects to admire; their real value is in their find spot and in particular how they relate to the 'known' archaeological record – the much larger resource from which artefacts are drawn. Recent research by Katie Robbins, Tom Brindle and Philippa Walton, among others, has highlighted the tremendous contribution that accurately reported finds can make to our understanding of the archaeology of England and Wales. Part of Dr Brindle's work focussed on Roman-period finds from North Lincolnshire; these contributed twenty-nine new sites – an increase of 21 per cent in the region. Dr Robbins brought further clarity to the significance of PAS data by exploring the different sources of bias contained within them. Bias affects all archaeological datasets, and without due consideration it can cause false patterns to emerge from the data. Robbins found bias existed in seven key areas – burial/loss, preservation, survival, exposure, recovery, reporting and recording. Robbins has shown that their impact is regionally variable – a crucial finding for a county with such a diverse landscape as Lincolnshire.

New sites, new stories
A similar exercise to that undertaken by Brindle and Robbins was undertaken by the author for Lincolnshire PAS data. Owing to the complexity of archaeological datasets, comparing PAS data to the known archaeological record is not an easy task, but at a very basic level it was possible to establish that a significant proportion of finds reported to PAS come from sites that we previously knew nothing about. For most periods this ranged between 60 per cent and 80 per cent of all finds – new sites being those that fell more than 300 m away from existing sites. These new sites dramatically increase the total number of sites known about; for the medieval period we now have 23 per cent more sites, while for the Anglo-Saxon period PAS data increases the total number by 64 per cent. Of course, these trends vary tremendously across the different landscapes encountered in Lincolnshire.

North Lincolnshire Finds Liaison Officer Martin Foreman holding the 'Glentham kettle'.

Not all objects discovered in situ are old. This bronze vessel was discovered by a metal detectorist at Glentham. The finder stopped digging and called the archaeologists when the top of the vessel appeared. At first it resembled an Iron Age bronze vessel, but it quickly turned out to be a kettle from the Second World War.

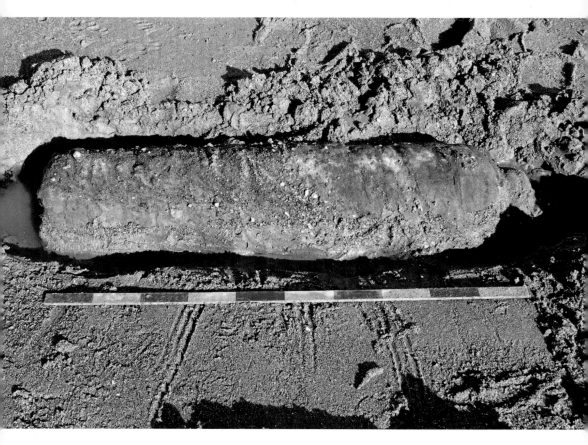

This object caused a bit of a stir when it emerged from the beach near Skegness. It was found by a lady walking along the beach who reported it as possible cannon. When we arrived we were concerned that it could be an exploded bomb, but it quickly became clear it was just a rusted gas cylinder.

Place, as it was argued earlier, is an intimate outworking of landscape and people. PAS data highlights this nuanced relationship rather well.

Most artefact scatters are, however, comprised of finds from different periods. Indeed, in Lincolnshire 93 per cent of finds form multi-period assemblages. These scatters are temporally chaotic, with various chronological combinations reflecting both the repeated use of particular places, but also a range of depositional and post-depositional factors. In spite of bias, which affects all datasets regardless of how they are recovered, finds reported to the PAS are important biographical components of the landscape. In some cases finds recovered through metal detecting are the sole witness to activity in a certain period. At Sudbrooke, near Lincoln, a large Roman villa excavated between 2005 and 2007 revealed a settlement which began as a typical small-scale rural farmstead comprising a series of timber structures and land divisions. These were later rebuilt in a more elaborate fashion, incorporating mosaic floors, a hypocaust system, and painted wall plaster. The stone building was apparently abandoned in the late second or third century, with robbing of the walls being carried out into the late third century.

No evidence for occupation after the demolition of the stone building was discovered through excavation, and the site has a complete absence of pottery dating to the fourth century. In order to gain further information, a metal-detecting survey of the plough zone was organised. The results were astounding; very little evidence for the period during which the villa was occupied was found. Rather, the majority of finds indicated significant activity in the later third and fourth centuries – a period for which the excavation was silent. The likely reason for this is that all of the evidence for later activity has now been destroyed by ploughing. Had the plough-soil not been investigated, this crucial evidence would have been missed. The Roman villa at Sudbrooke highlights just how important it is to combine different types of evidence in order to understand archaeological sites better.

Excavation of a Roman villa at Sudbrooke. Metal detecting of the plough zone was combined with excavation in order to retrieve a greater range of evidence.

Roman tile from a hypocaust. This was found reused in a middle Saxon settlement. It was presumably robbed from a Roman villa in the region.

Final remarks

The archaeology of Lincolnshire, as we have glimpsed through these fifty finds, is diverse, illuminating and enriches our sense of place. Yet it is also precious, not just in a material sense, but more importantly in that it is a finite resource. We must preserve it, care for it, love it, steward it and report it. It has been said elsewhere that a find is only truly discovered once it has been recorded, and this is the ethos of the Portable Antiquities Scheme. By systematically recording these discoveries – regardless of how well preserved or complete they are – we can continue to understand our common past better. With every turn of the spade there is the potential to unearth new information, but this information can only be fully realised through recording.

If you wish to find out more about these finds please visit our website www.finds.org. uk. Here you can also find information on best practice, recording, conservation and even volunteering with the Portable Antiquities Scheme.